Mama Used to Say...

LaMario D. Garrett

Contents

Dedication

Ethel Mae Garrett

1922-2004

This book is dedicated to our grandmother, Ethel Mae Garrett. She was born in the red clay hills of Flat Rock Fayetteville, Ga. Her mother a Cherokee Indian and her father who was Bi-Racial had dreams for their nine children.

This was most taxing in the south that was heated with racial prejudice. Despite all of it, our mama, as we called her, marched as a pioneer for the civil rights movement. Her march however was on the pavements of the hearts of her children, and she left a mark.

Her story is no different from that of many others, and so this book is dedicated not only to her but also to all

Of the grandmothers, the nanas, mamas, grandmas and big mammas or whatever you may call yours all over the world.

Without all of you, a lot of us would be lost. Compiled in these pages are the poems and short stories

That are the markings of our mother's influence on my life; these are the things that she said.
"God could not be everywhere so, he created Grandmothers."

This book is also dedicated to my little sister Kenyetta Cohen who recently passed away right before this book was published.

About The Author

Born June 7, 1979, LaMario Garrett was the eldest of five children born to his mother Jan Garrett. Like most young boys, he was abandoned by his father and was denied at birth. He sought solace in his Grandmother for peace. Although his mother was present and very active in his life, he gravitated to the love of his seasoned grandmother.

Suffering Molestation at an early age, would lead LaMario down a rollercoaster like life, this would inspire this and another book. He graduated from Georgia Perimeter College with an Associate degree in Journalism and currently works at one of Atlanta's Law firm's as a Mail Courier.

He now resides in Fayetteville, Ga the place his grandmother was born, with his family.

Special thanks to the following for all of their assistance
with the creation of this book.

Asta Moore, Editor
Felicia Smith, Editor
Charles Warner, Legal Advisor
Rod Dreyer, Designer
Dennis Glass, Illustrator
Joyce Hargette, Administration

WHO SHOULD READ THIS BOOK

"IF YOU HAVE HAD TO BEAR EVERYTHING

TO BELIEVE IN SOMETHING, JUST TO HAVE
ANYTHING

OR IF YOU HAVE ENDURED EVRYTHING, WELL
PERHAPS YOU NEED TO READ THIS BOOK".

-the Author

WHAT YOU WILL LEARN FROM THIS BOOK

The secret to life is not promised in these pages nor is riches and glory. What I do promise is that somewhere in one of the short stories or in at least one of the poems you might see your sentiments. I promise you will find hope, education from ignorance and yes peace within yourself for whatever your plight is in life. This I can promise to you the reader"

-the Publisher

Momma
used to
say...

MY FRIEND

I MISS YOUR FACE,
WITH ITS ENCHANTING GRACE.

YOU'RE DAUNTING SMILE
THAT MAKES HAPPINESS LINGER FOR MORE
THAN A WHILE.

HOW I LONG TO HEAR YOUR HEALING VOICE,
WHICH INHABITS MY INHIBITIONS AND
HELPS MY CHANCES, MAKE THE CHOICE.

OH, HOW I LONG TO SEE YOU AGAIN, MY FRIEND.

SPRING'S SWEET MORNINGS ARE NEVER AS
SWEET AS YOU.

HAPPY SUMMER DAYS WOULD ENVY ALL
THE SMILES

WE KNEW JUST FROM KNOWING YOU.

WINTER'S CHILL COULD NOT EPITOMIZE

MY BROKEN HEART'S CALL,

FOR SINCE, YOU WENT AWAY; MY TEARS
RESEMBLE AUTUMN'S LEAVES THAT
FALL.
I GUESS, THOUGH, FOR NOW I'LL LIVE
OFF MY MEMORIES UNTIL THE BITTER
END,
GOODBYE FOR NOW, UNTIL I SEE YOU AGAIN
MY FRIEND.

Ethel

I was incredibly blessed to have made so important a friend as Ethel, even before I was old enough to understand what friendship meant. As a baby, all I knew was that there was a, beautiful woman with dark skin loving me in the same way that my mother loved me.

What I came to understand about this friendship — as I got older — was that Ethel's love for me came as a natural result of a friendship that was in place long before I arrived in the picture. I'm talking about the bond between my mother and Ethel. Privately each spoke of the other to me with such respect and dignity. In time, Ethel and I established our own personal connection that was unlike any I would ever again know.

I could make her laugh with a silly dance I'd made up, and I performed this dance often simply because I felt better when I heard her laugh. You all know the sound of it. That rolling muffled laugh deep in her chest that made her almost start coughing and caused her eyes to close and her face to wrinkle in total glee.

To make her laugh was perhaps my most powerful talent as a

boy, because it simply created good feelings in our house. Ethel could change a room just by being in it make it lighter without even opening the curtains.

When she worked, she hummed. Never in a hurry. Never wasting time. Never overlooking what needed to be done. She cared about us, our house, her work. She had that beautiful and rare gift of being content with whatever task she was doing. For this reason alone, I consider her one of the most successful people I have ever known. She was ahead of all of our family in this respect.

I have never known anyone who took so much pleasure in pleasing others. Ethel would have been a Class A nurse, But it really didn't matter what she called her job description. She was a contributor. She made other lives better.

When my grandfather brought Ethel into our lives by giving her a job at the laundry (he called her "Shorty"), no one could have guessed then the many ways our lives would be made better. Even if you just consider the cleaning aspect of her work. That's no small thing to keep everything clean ... floors, bathrooms, ovens, clothes. She made the old adage "Cleanliness is next to Godliness" come alive, because I could see that she believed it. She took such pride in it. Even as a child, because of her, I came to respect cleanliness and see it as a state of clarity that we should expect and maintain for ourselves,

Once when I was desperately trying to clean up a stain for which I knew I was in big trouble, she walked in the room and saw my failed efforts. I was wondering what special chemical I needed to find to reverse this disaster.. Ethel got down with me on the floor with a rag, soap and warm water. Her strong arms started in with their cleaning magic. I'll never forget what she said. "There's nothing you can't clean up without soap and water and hard scrubbing," I watched her make my crime disappear. It was watching her confident effort that stayed in my mind I think of her every time I am scrubbing at some stain and I smile. And I never give up.

Because I grew up in a house where a woman of color was loved and she loved us back, my world defied the broader world of the South where ignorance bred racial prejudice. I simply never bought into it. I had living proof of the insanity of all that. I have Ethel to thank for that.

Ethel and I had nicknames for one another. As my grandfather did, she called me "Markie-Boy" , and later "Marco." From a long way back, I called her "Eppie" ... later shortened to "Epp" when I became a teenager. To you this name will sound strange, no doubt. But for Epp and me it was as natural as the sound of breathing. Using those names as we did was just like saying "I love you" every time we used them. Though we also shared those three words regularly, especially as I grew to be a young man. Then an older one.

The next to last time I saw her, there was just a moment of recognition in her face. I was so grateful for that, because I knew she was losing touch with her past. Then the last time I saw her, I was a stranger. The sadness of this was a challenge for me, as it was for all of you, I am sure. I felt a great loss. I realized that part of what I liked about myself was that Ethel liked me. Without that recognition, I felt a piece of me back away into a shadow. I wasn't really sure how to handle it. I feel some shame about not going back to see her ... as if I had already allowed her to die. But I didn't know how to do it. The awful feeling of being in her presence as a stranger was so disheartening.

Had it been me losing my grasp on reality, Ethel would have been there...doing things for me... regardless of what I could or could not understand. I am sure of that. She was a better person than I am. But this I know...1 am a better person for having known her. I will never forget her. Great people live on through others. Ethel was...is...one of great people.

If ever I need to feel calmness and security, all I need do is think of her ironing at a board. I can smell the warm clothes. Hear the hiss of the iron. She is humming quietly. So satisfied that she is doing a perfect thing.

By Markie boy
(Mark Warren)

"A Child's Molester's Nursery Rhyme"

There once was a lady who lived in the forest,
a child molester she was and her name was Doris.
She touched little boys where she never should.
Most tried to get away, but never could
she gained the trust of the boy's closet kin,
And that's how her rhyme begins.

"Hi Ms. so & so. You say you need to go to the store.
Leave the boy with me," she says, as she closes the door.
"Come closer my child, don't be afraid. I'm your friend",
the molester says.

"Let's play a little game; this is how it goes, stand on your
tip toes,"
"Ms. Doris what big hands you have", the boy, says,
as she pulls him near. "Ms. Doris what large legs you
have",
She says "all the more to squeeze you with my dear",

Oh Ms. Doris, what have you done to those boys,
you made them play with your body parts as they would
their little toys.
Didn't you think how it would affect them? As their spongy
little minds grew,
or did you even consider what would happen if their

families knew.
How do you think they'll turn out Ms. Doris, those boys
you perverted so young? Let's
see if they turned out right or wrong.

Some will remember what you did and come to hate all
women the same,
they'll beat and abuse women and even call them out of
their name.
There might be a few who will trust you because their
fathers were not there anyway,
they may not understand sex at all and my guess is they
will end up gay.
You'll have a couple who will adjust to their sick, perverted
minds,
and these will be the ones who to will grow
to have a molester's rhyme.

I wonder if they'll be one who will get past the hurt
someday,
who'll write a poem like this one and forgive you anyway.
Yes, you'll mess up a lot of families' lives, in so many
ways.
Ms. Doris you might even screw up their children's' mind.
Your venom will surely reach beyond their days.
Molestation causes a horrible cycle; rape goes with it, hand
in hand.
You should tell all those children the truth

Ms. Doris; you're the real boogey-man.

Watch out all you unsuspecting parents, keep your little
boys close.
Tick-tock, it's a matter of time,
The one you hold close, just might have a dose of
"A Child's Molester's Nursery Rhyme".

THE LESSON

"It's just a matter of time before he realizes that I'm his son and he'll come back for both of us you'll see." Mason shouted at his mother Ava as he stormed down the hall and slammed the door. Ava sat back, as she forced the last bit of chardonnay down. She exhaled deeply and began to speak aloud to herself. "How da hell did I end up here? John told me we were going to be together. This is the only reason I had Mason, and now I got a little girl too. What da hell was I thinking; and to think he married that bitch Vaughn. I only hope my baby girl Madison won't be like me." Ava gathered herself out of the chair slowly. She walked down the hall, which seemed to take forever; she laid her head gently against Mason's door. And said, "Mason please open the door and let's talk about this baby." "Not now Ava, I'm praying. Go away", the childish voice exclaimed from behind the door. Ava softly shed tears, wandering why Mason still called her by her first name.

"What's wrong with our boy?" a voice resounded behind Ava. "Mama you scared me." Ava said as she turned around. There stood this woman who resembled the epitome of motherhood, Ms. Bessie, who was half Cherokee Indian. She stood stately with pecan skin and long flowing hair, a large full belly that jiggled when she laughed. An eminent and enchanting presence that claimed little Mason's love and his heart so much that he called her mama. To him the name seemed to fit his grandmother. "Masoonn, say amen to God and open this door for me". It only took a second before the door flung open and this dark wide-eyed boy leaped out into Bessie's arm. "Maaama", little Mason yelled with a smile the size of Texas on his face. "I'm still praying to God for a daddy but it seems there's no answer. Do you think he's busy mama or maybe he's just said no, whatchu think?"

"I think that God gives us what we need when we need it. It's like a card game Mason. The winner is not determined by the hand he has been dealt. Do you know what does?" "I know, I know, its how you play the hand you have been dealt". "You got it", Ms Bessie said. "Besides if God never gives you a daddy, He has promised to be a father to the fatherless. And who can ask for a better father than that?" "I guess you're right, I will just do what you taught me, I will wait on the Lord." "Mason how about helping me get your granddaddy's supper on the table?" Mason looked wide-eyed up to his grandmother Bessie. He then reached out grabbing his mother Ava's hand, and said, "What we got for granddaddy to eat?" He said as they went quietly down hall. Ms. Bessie looked down and smiled and said, "we got yams, neck bones and cabbage with a lil bit of ho-cake bread. What you think about that? "Mason says, 'I think granddaddy will say, "Dems good eats."

"Black Man"

In the beginning, God above
created the heavens and the earth,
and from the latter, with labor pains,
I was given birth.

The clay of Africa produced
my ways, and out of the dusty sand,
I emerged with strength and vigor
as the specimen, called a black man.

I withstood the Sun's great heat

The moonlit sky revealed my stride,

Posed for my body to get beat, I stood tall with my Queen
as my pride.

There were some who hung my kind on trees.
I stood tall though, I would not fall,
for there were lessons from the least of these.
Enslaved, I've been there,

sold and drowned at the southern stream.
With tears in my eyes and chains at my thighs,
I still had a dream.

I envisioned a time when the black man
wouldn't be measured by those in the prison's residence,
for it doesn't define me, because I am told the other day
they made a black man president.

To some I am an animal,
others call me a nigger,
but I rise above the petty name calling
because I figure,
that like it or not I'm here to stay, I will excel above the
rest.
I've been given no choice, I have to fight harder than others,
I must be the best.

The shackles are broken, the
dust has settled and triumphantly I still stand,
quite more than phenomenal, I am the image of God,

I Am A Black Man.

"Misunderstood"

My Presence offends those who try to watch me from
within.
Sometimes I pretend to comprehend their inability
to capture my essence that never bends. You cannot gauge it,
my friend.

I am misunderstood.

Stop trying to figure out my swagger, because none of your
opinions of me really matter. My greatness you see only gets
fatter and fatter, when your envious
chatter, pitter-patters.
Have you experienced the epiphany's clatter? Let me
simplify,

I am misunderstood

Maybe it all appears too deep, but you cannot deny the love
that emanates from me to those I meet.
My personality is familiar to all the newly ones that I
choose to greet.
This kind of being cannot be grasped; it is like trying to hold wet

wood.
You couldn't hold my personality even if you could, although perhaps
you should.
And now I must close, for the eager to explain, me, brings woes
upon woes

My intellect knows, that, that's the way the world goes and
I suppose it's all good,

And just like the dots after this last line

I am………………………. Misunderstood.

The Family

The other day I was thinking of our generation.
A group, an offspring from seeds of long ago.

Some are gone, I thought with somber meditation,
but still we stand to watch our younger seedlings grow.

Those seeds blossom, in time that passes quickly
the world snatches some before we are aware

But this pedigree we've been entrusted gains the victory,
in adoration we leave our adversaries to stare.

My hope is that all the stead will find and take their place
on this road where our forefathers fought for us to be.

May each of us except our plight in this life with grace,
and stand united in victory as the family.

REJECTION

Does he like me?
Is she my type?
Or will she chew the game I spit?
I hope he believes the hype.

I bet she'll think I am ugly.
Can I get him to accept my weight?
If he says no,
I'll just die or run and hide
behind my fears I'll vacate.

Fear of rejection rings
these questions from us deep within,
it makes us lose faith in ourselves
and that my friend is a sin.

It discourages our inhibitions
from those we want to get to know.
It stifles our potential to
plant the seed of love to grow.

Every relationship started with a question,

just imagine if your
mom and dad did not try,
if they did not get pass their
questions of when and why.

I was told, "Nothing comes to a dreamer but sleep"
so don't just wish and hope for the best.
Grab your chance for love,
your right to happiness.

And if they say no just remember,
"There's many fish in the sea,
that have never been caught."
There is no love in fear, and
true love must be sought

Flowers

Budded peddles stand
Blossom now with grace
Bestowed upon you is prettiness
It's love upon your face
You wind, blow now upon her rosemary hair,
Not too heavy, you must blow with care.
Summer and spring, you are her husband.
Taste her kind gentle touch.
You rain, please feed her beauty,
but be careful, not too much.
And as she dies and is reborn,
you valleys try not to envy her ability
to grasp your depth and not be torn.
You mountains do not be jealous
of how high I let her tower,
for l am God Almighty
and this is my gift to all creation,
My Flower.

"ONCE"

My heart fell once;
it danced to the beat of love
and graced even the shadows of enchantment
over emptiness I hovered above

I laughed once
as I was tickled with youth and its adolescent embrace,
gosh did I feel time stand still the first time I saw your
face.

I exploded too numerous to count
as we shared each other's peace
when sounds of empty talkers ceased and deceased.

I cried once
when I could feel our love couldn't last,
for it was "wrong"
built on fallacies that we had to learn to let pass.

Therefore, in that moment, in that time, my heart lay
dormant for weeks upon months
because I had cried and laughed,
but my love died.
My heart ran for cover to hide
because I loved you once

"FLY FOR ME"

Stretch Out 'Your Wings; Spread Them High for the entire world to see

FLY FOR ME, My Dear Sisters and Brother, FLY FOR ME

You are most beautiful young <u>Kenyatta,</u> your body is weak, but you are strong,

Look at you — happy and married --.with Michael you will not go wrong

Dig deep down inside, find ˉyour wealth, you've come too far, don't look back, keep ahead

I don't care what anyone tells you, you will be happy, remember now, what I've said

'This most handsome male child has grown up, stand on
your feet young Curtis you are now a man
If anyone can make it through this cruel cold world; surely you
can. The time is now for you to claim your

Birth right, shine like the Eastern Star just remember young
brother, and do not forget, who's, whom and whose'n you
really are.

And now the baby of this cute bunch, my message to you is
short and sweet, it's only with the help of the true God; will
you these feelings defeat

Cenisha, your stride is graceful; your beauty tasteful; it's no
wonder you're desired by all but remember, unless you're
desired by God on high, all your aspirations will fall
'you are the most like me, I know you well please, heed
this advice, you can win this cruel game called life,
But it's all in the way you roll, your dice

I'm so proud of you all. For we are a most unusual' clan and although we have been thrown many obstacles still like true champions we stand. A body of siblings unlike no other, listen carefully my sisters and brother stretch out your wings, spread them high for this entire world to see.

Up, up and away, higher and higher that's it –

FLY FOR ME, FLY FOR ME

What will be said at my funeral
the day that I'm laid to rest,
when the enemy death ensues my body,
and my heart is stilled in my chest.

The day my friends and loved ones
have come to say their goodbyes,
just what would I like to hear
if I could, on the day I come to die.

Do not praise my outgoing character,
or my ability to sing.
Please don't mention the book I wrote
no, no not that sort of thing.

A room full of mourners won't impress me,
for I'll be gone on that day.
The flowers can be kept to yourselves
I cannot smell them anyway.

My love for my family should have spoken for itself.
Don't save it for praise of me on that day,
it really would not matter much at all
what men thought or might say.

I only hope and pray when I come to die,
my accolades of life will come from God on high.
When I am taken away, I hope it is just for a while,
and the life I led, I hope it will be received
by God with a smile.

So at my funeral, at the end of my race,
when my course to the finish has been run,
I only long to hear the awaited promise
for the Lord to say, "Well done".

A BOY AND HIS GRANDMAMA

A sleeping boy was awakened, for his sweet dreams were quickly taken.

By a nightmare, he had in his head; you see he dreamed his grandmama was dead.

So out of bed that poor child hopped, to the floor with his knees he dropped.

and cried out "Lord don't let this be," Let my grandma always stay with me.

As you can see, that boy loved his grandma hard, for she gave love to him right from the start.

He watched, as she feed the poor, sheltered the homeless

And to the sick never closed her door.

He appreciated how she use to pray,

and oh, how he wanted to grow to be like her someday.

Deep down inside she taught him to give, to die to himself daily

and in addition, in turn help others to live.
He loved how he would climb in her bed,

and how there with her, he remained free from dread.

With "Amen", he ended the prayer on his knees,
His grandma's voice set his soul at ease.
She told him, "Come get in the bed with me

For sleeping here, you'll feel better, you'll see.

and there they lay, free from drama,

That boy and his grandmamma.
However, when the boy awoke on the next day,

He knew the reality and everything wasn't okay
You see the night before was really a dream,

and the nightmare was, as it seemed.

His grandmama wasn't asleep in the bed, she was dead.

As he climbed out of bed, he noticed his legs and hands,

They were much bigger; this boy was really a man.

You see, through the years he could not come to grips with his grief,
the poor boy remained in utter disbelief.

Oh, he tried so very hard to live.

The more he tried, the more he longed for the love only his grandma could give.

He reached out to people with his thoughts, but no comfort to him was truly brought.

He longed, loved and grieved too hard, and the only one who could help was God.

and so it was in his bed one day his family found that poor child,

For it was there one spring morning he died with a smile.

His family did not shed tears you see, for they knew this is where he wanted to be.

It didn't quite make sense, they tried hard to understand, why there was so much pain in just one man. He never understood it himself,

He shed his tears to his thoughts and no one else. A sad story to some this might seem, but the boy finally achieved his dream.

To sleep with her always free from dread, away from all of life's nightmare drama, and that's where they lay down to this day, that boy and his grandmamma.

ETHAN: THE CHILD

He arose from the ashes,
a silhouette of combined organisms
that thrashes together matter into a colossal being
which latches and attaches to
a specimen called you Ethan, the child.

The miracle of your life
held together by your mother,
who was willing to sacrifice her existence.
Who prayed with due diligence and persistence.
She defied her body's resistance and all for you Ethan, the
child.

Tears swell as I attempt to tell your tale,
of a mother who loved you so very well,
that she put her life on the line
so that you can be given time,
space to laugh, live and shine,
to grow, to love and dance and say this life is mine.

And all these thoughts made her smile,
because she could finally say
I've been given a son for a while.

The dance of a mother that she will waltz with style.
just imagine all her love is for you Ethan, the child.

Mama Used to Say

Over the hills and through the valleys life experiences
take you from day to day,

"But you got to hold your own right or wrong"
that's what Mama used to say.

I thought all her sayings were wise;
however, I never cared to really listen,
they were old women tales, I thought, that did not seem
important
enough to pay attention.

I am older now and I apply those "silly" words
that Mama used to say.

My life has proven "I'm not the little boy who sat
his apples down; I sold'em", without delay
I have beat all the odds, overcame the struggles.
I won the breaks, held the family together.
Forgave the unforgivable,

Fought fights that were unbelievable.

I have cried because of what people said,
when my haters wanted me dead.
It was her words that rang loud in my ears,
her face that stood proud in all of my tears.
I heard, "Nothing comes to a dreamer but sleep,
But you stand tall on both your feet.
Beat those odds; win this life, not tomorrow but today",
Thank God above for all of those words that my mama
used to say.

"The Long Road Home"

Aries grabbed his grandmother's hand and escorted her into the apartment. It was humble; nevertheless, it was home, their new home. Although Aries hated their new living conditions, he realized that it was a good move. A step away from the distractions that made him feel as if his life was spiraling over a precipice of doom and destruction. You see, he had lived the last 6 years of his life in a relationship with a man. His name was Cedric. Aries figured he loved him, but he always felt torn. His religious upbringing and his discontent did not allow him peace. He believed and saw the evidence of God and wanted to change, despite society's efforts to sway him to stay, gay. Therefore, he left Cedric; this would be his start   to please God and find happiness for himself.

While helping his grandmother to bed, there was a knock at the door. When he made his way to open the door, there stood a gorgeous specimen of the female anatomy. Her name was Kim. A beautiful bi-racial, petite young lady who flung her flowing hair over her shoulders and spoke so gently, "I noticed you and your grandmother moving in; I thought it was so cool seeing you with her and well, I wondered if y'all needed some help settling in". After Aries caught his breath and stopped his fast beating heart, he invited her in. You see, Aries was very much attracted to females but was never given a chance to love one and he did want so badly to marry and have a family.

Inside Aries and Kim sat down and talked for hours about their lives and their compatibilities. The highlight of the conversation, however, was the thoughts shared about their grandmothers who raised each of them. Everyday afterwards for months Kim came over to help Aries with his grandmother who seemed to be quite fond of Kim, and every night after that they put Aries' grandmother to bed and they would just talk until the early morning. It was those sacred moments that confirmed their individual thoughts of one another and that was that they were hopelessly and unequivocally in love with each other.

After sometime, however, the inevitable happened. Late one night while he was putting his grandmother to bed, Aries received an unexpected visitor. It was Cedric he stood at the door begging to be let in. Cedric was a handsome down-low brother who loved to reappear in Aries' life when it was most inconvenient for Aries. "Are you gonna just let me stand out here? Aries, I miss you", Cedric exclaimed. "Let me in". Aries took a deep breath mustard up the courage and said, "you know, my grandmother said you would do this, Cedric. She said you would wait until I found some real happiness and just like the devil himself, you would strike. But not this time buddy. It is not going to work. Cedric, I am fighting for my right to be happy and to be free from all the pain that life has caused me. Do not speak, just leave, and just like that, he was gone.

As Aries closed the door, his grandmother's voice and presence calmed the uneasy mood. "On the road of life, Aries," his grandmother said, "there will always be twists and turns, hills, and even some muddy puddles that we just might step in. They can make a mess, but Aries, the point is not where you started on that road, not the travels, but what matters is where you end up, and you determine that, baby. If you're blessed, you'll end up home". She kissed him on his forehead and quietly said goodnight and started down the hallway. Just then, the doorbell rang, and an excited voice on the other side made Aries light up with joy. His grandmother turned and said, "Aries open the door chile, let her in, you're home now baby, your home".

"WATCH YOUR FRIENDS"

When I was a boy, I sat on my grandmother's knee.
She began to regale me with the ins and outs
of life and how it could be.

I was told to keep an eye on my enemies,
and If I did I'd know how to fight
their envies from within.
She told me that was the easy part though,
what I really had to do was watch those I chose to call a
friend.

"A friend you see," she said, as she held me ever near,

"Is allowed by you to understand what makes your tick to
tock
and what causes even your tear to fear".

"Now you betta watch real close, "That ole lady said. "Cause
your so called friend could be holding a ghost, that might
wanna see your best and most, dead".

Oh, they can smile in your face, but you- -you watch your

back,
that's where some of them put their knife.
Their jealousies could fight to fill your life with cool ice,
that cause strife that I promise won't be nice.

"Is it possible to have true friends?" I asked my grandmother
who knew.

She told me, "real and true friends ain't like money honey,
one or two often will do."

I asked, "how is it possible to watch and find a real confidant,
who'll go with you to the very end?"
She smiled and whispered,
"That's where the wisdom comes in,
because you'll see you never, ever have to watch a true
friend."

THIRTY SOMETHING

I turned thirty the other day, and you know it is funny, for the first time I could admit age, my age that is. The precipice from which I dangled daily because of the inevitability of age, and death disappeared. In addition, it was in that moment, that I experienced an epiphany an enlightenment, if you will. You see for the first time, people became real to me and the actual process of living was assured within me.

I was grown, not only in age but also in reality. There was no more mama to hold my hand or to tell me, as only she could that 'everything would be alright'. She was gone now. I am sure some one out there knows what I am talking about. The world was cruel now that she was gone but she had given me the tools to take it and to make it in this life. Tyrone Davis said it best when he said 'I've reached a turning point in my life' and I had and you know what I liked it.

My past was just that, my past.

I wished the world would have left it there. When they looked back, I looked back, at all of my mistakes, all of my shortcomings. Therefore, because of that fact I could not process the growth needed. That ended at thirty, I was grown. If a person could not leave my mistakes in the past well then piss on them, 'Cry to tears in the bucket, mutherfuckit' that's what mama used to say. I liked me and I wasn't going to apologize any more for being me, I didn't have to and to be frank I didn't want to.

I had also learned that while family was good some gave more than others did in the family circle. Some took and never gave and some just made you cry because you gave until it hurt. If this occurs in your family do not get upset or disgruntle, just wait to let them see there error. Mama used to say 'children, they go from the knee to the heart; what makes you laugh one day might make you cry'. You see they will have children of there own that will teach them far better than you or I ever could. Therefore, as for my family and me, I hush listen and wait. I watch and see everything that mama said unfolds. I wonder if they do though.

It seemed like yesterday that all of us were children playing outside, eating watermelon and frolicking through the fields of College Park, that was were I was raised, you know. Yes, indeed I am College Park raised, College Park born and when I die, I'll be College Park gone. There, everyone was family and everyone knew my grandmother Ms Ethel Mae Garrett. 2205 West Columbia Ave that was mama's address. On Saturdays, the streets were alive with people. Mama sat on her front porch as she shucked corn while Uncle Sam played his blues harmonica as the neighborhood danced to the music that came from that porch. College Park was, is, and always will be home to me. It's funny; I can still hear us laughing, my cousin Doc and me, jumping and being little boys. Living young with an innocence and peace with life. Someone out there has to feel what I am saying.

Christmas time at mamas was the joys of my childhood. The smell of pine mingled with the cooked turkey in the oven and the glistening tree in the living room with presents everywhere. Bells were indeed ringing the glad news as we sang Carla Thomas 'Gee Wiz it's Christmas. Yea, it was nice, growing up as a child.

I finally understood that I did not want to leave all that behind and could you blame me. Once I realized I was grown though, it seemed that I became cool with the process of change and growth. I finally accepted saying good-bye to that little boy with his wide-eyed fantasies of life. Good-bye to mama, goodbye to yester year. I realized then that although I was grown, it was okay to sometimes remember. I knew it was okay to always remember all the things that I have been taught, to live. And it only took about 28, 29 – yea did I tell you that I turned thirty the other day and you know to me that   is so, so funny.

STRUGGLE

I see you watching me because I am watching you too

Trying to see if your eyes caught a glimpse of the hidden
truth

You see this rise I got in my pants, is hard for me to
understand,

I cannot explain the excitement in my belly when I see you

another man

I struggle

This shit is a struggle I am trying hard though to put it to
rest

They say its mind over matter and so I put this theory to
test

I struggle

I would not wish this on my most hated enemy

death would be better for me,

Why would one choose a life like this?

Its utter misery you see

I struggle

I will not act on my feelings for God would be hurt,

In addition, how can I approach him in prayer?

I would feel worst than dirt

Therefore, as for this struggle I will keep fighting until he
says I am through.

Yeah I see you watching me because I am watching you
too.

No, No, Not You

I had always hoped to dance to the symphony of love

A gliding chance of romance

A glistening blessing from above

I had always dreamed of what she would look like

and I could see her warm brown skin

Her beating heart with a humble pace

That came from deep within

But, I never knew that love could hurt and burn like this

I am left mad as hell yeah you heard me well

I'm really pissed!

You see I gave up so much for you

and you never gave in return,

all I can say this has been a bitch

and a lesson well learned

However, I know I will dance the dance of love

and my dream of romance will one day come true

But I must accept in my heart of hearts

That this dream and dance just won't be with you

Have You Ever?

Have you ever danced the dance of the dervish?

Or waltzed to the Tennessee?

Have you ever peered into the night's deep sky?

Or wondered what God might be?

Have you loved until it hurts?

Or cried until the tears subsided?

Have you ever been granted the favor of good family?

Where real love lingered and resided?

Or what of passion, did you ever experience its flavor

Where it soon arose, and then it ceased?

Answer, did you know breathtaking lovemaking and its finale

the release?

Did you live? Have you laughed?

The answer to these questions should be graced with a yes and not a never.

And yet, I still ask to you, the reader of this poem well, have you ever?

"I Got It"

An old woman was sweeping on her front porch one day, when she noticed a girl on the street.

She was just 'a crying, wailing back and forth and with her hands her chest she did beat.

The old woman approached carefully and put her hand on the young girl to calm her distress.

Gently she asked, "What's the matter baby?" "You seem to be such a mess".

The young girl told the old woman she had been to the doctor and found out she was going to die.

She couldn't figure out why she had been given a disease-- she just wanted to know the reason why.

What the old woman told the girl next was quite difficult for the girl to swallow.

She asked, "If the doctor told you that you were going to die, "what did he tell you that you did not already know?"

"You should've known before you went to see that doctor that you were going to die.''

But, sometimes we fool ourselves child about death, to ourselves we lie".

"We're each on a road that has a final destination with death, so don't feel sorry for yourself,

do like most of us do, enjoy life, learn its lessons and focus your attention on its true wealth."

You see, we all are dying every day, healthy or not we all have the same way to go". "

Don't matter the age, be it young or old, we must recognize and know,

That it's not the years, but what you do with them that determines if you really really can say,

That you beat all the odds come what may, that you fought the fine fight every inch of the way".

Understand this, despite what you were told, remember you didn't die today,

and the doctor is not God. You still have time to live, for it is time that has the final say."

"You are going to die of this I am certain," the old woman said as she finished her vent. "But try living each day one at a time, do you get it'?"

The young girl said, yes ma'am, "I got it."

Heart to Heart

TWO BROTHERS WERE TALKING AND
THE CONVERSATION TURNED MAD,

YOU SEE THE YOUNGER HATED
THE ELDER
FOR THE POSITION TIIAT HE
HAD.

"YOUR SPEECH AND YOUR
DRESS ARE
QUITE ANNOYING TO ME,"

THE YOUNGER STATED TO HIS SENIOR, WHO
SAT IN DISBELIEF,

ONE THING AFTER ANOTHER THE
YOUNGER SPOKE WHAT HE HATE.

"I EVEN HATE HOW YOU SLEEP

AND WHEN YOU EAT THE SOUNDS
THAT YOU MAKE.

YOU THINK YOU KNOW EVERYTHING AND

BECAUSE YOU'RE OLDER YOU HAVE THE STRENGTH,

BUT THE TRUTH IS I'M FASTER AND I'M BIGGER
WITH BETTER LOOKS AND LONGER LENGTH."
WITH TEARS IN HIS EYES THE ELDER BEGAN TO SAY,
"THIS HAS TRULY BEEN ENLIGHTENING,[DIDN'T
KNOW YOU FELT THIS WAY.

YOU SEE, WHEN THEY BROUGHT YOU HOME AS A BABY
I WAS YOUR PROTECTOR AND FRIEND,
I VOWED TO ALWAYS BE THERE FOR YOU
AND TO DO IT RIGHT TO THE END.

AS YOU GREW, I KNEW YOU'D BE MORE
HANDSOME THAN I,

AND YOUR GREATER STRENGHT WAS QUITE CLEAR,
BUT I NEVER ASK THE LORD WHY?

AND SO YOU THINK I KNOW IT ALL,

YOU'VE GOT IT QUITE WRONG.

IT'S YOU WITH THE KNOWLEDGE, I JUST

DANCE, TO YOUR SONG.

AND IF YOU I HAVE OFFENDED,

THESE NEXT WORDS WILL AMEND IT.

WHILE YOU WERE WALKING IN MY SHADOW,

I WAS ADMIRING YOUR FAME,

IN THE BIBLE IT WAS THE ELDER THAT WERE
WEAKER REMEMBER ESAU AND CAIN."

AS THE YOUNGER BROTHER BEGAN TO CRY
FOR THE THINGS HE HAD SAID

THE ELDER EMBRACED HIM AND

AS HE LOVINGLY TOUCHED HIS HEAD
HE TOLD HIM "NEVER MIND THIS TALK AND JUST
LIKE THAT IT'S OVER AND DONE,

SOMETIMES WE HAVE TO LET OUR EMOTIONS
RUN
BUT JUST REMEMBER, LIKE GRANDMAMA SAID,
"TEETH AND TONGUE

FALL OUT, BUT THEY HANG IN THERE TOGETHER,
AND NO MATTER WHAT YOU DO

OR SAY, I'LL ALWAYS BE YOUR BIG BROTHER.

Depression

I wonder, in somber meditation

With eager pontification.

My hearts denial, for needed smiles.

But in my just unrest, I assess,

That I am utterly, bitterly, and emotionally depressed.

For no apparent reason or an unparticular season

A spaced out thought that my emotions caught

rendered this tighten feeling in my chest.

which brings this unrest and further it nests

my hearts cry, for it to be blessed,

While yet, it remains continually,

aggressively and chronically, depressed.

I cry, afraid to die, oh

Sometimes, though

My tears they chime, so

feelings of loneliness and disorderly bliss

seems to miss

The aggressions for p's obsession

while my refusal to learn life's hard lessons

which brings me the writer into

This recession

This regression

Hence the Depression.

"Mirror Mirror on the wall"

The other day, In the Mirror

I saw this sad boy, who cried for someone to save him,

He pleaded for my help, even begged for aid

But I grew afraid and so I delayed him.

His clothes were quite tattered he was abandoned you see

He exclaimed, look how this life has repaid me,

for I am but a child, I've been befuddled and beguiled,

I am as troubled as only a babe could be.

I dropped my head and covered my eyes, for the Mirror

served no longer a rejection,

for I knew the truth, it was no longer aloof, that

Mirrors only give reflection

Who will I tell? Who could set

the boy free by reaching inside of me to save him,

the other day, In the Mirror

I saw this sad boy, who cried for someone to save him,

"THE END"

It rained the night Mama died. All of her children and grandchildren flocked somberly to her bed where she lay in her white gown, her braids revealing her Indian background. We all knew of the certainty of her death one day, but we dreaded the fact that we were in that moment standing at the dawn of her demise. My brother Chris draped himself across her limp dying body with quiet tears, his face buried in her stomach as she gasped her last breaths. "Y'all be happy now for me", Mama said quietly, "I'll be at home soon." Mama took a gaze around her bed where she saw four generations of her seed, her family, standing with tears in their eyes, wondering different things, feeling different ways that amounted to sadness, helplessness, depravity and emptiness, put plainly, we were lost.

"Where will we go mama, how will we get by without you?" one of her grand¬daughters exclaimed, crying with sobs too deep to bear. The others chimed in with her in agreement. Mama, the mother of these generations, gathered her strength and spoke for the last time, "is that what I did? Did I make you so dependent on me rather than the things I tried to teach you? Death is a part of life, and you all will be here at this same deathbed someday. I wish I could go for you, but I can't. You'll have to meet God for yourself. I only hope when you do get here, you can look out and see what I see, cause I see a legacy of greatness that will remember all the things that they were taught to survive, to live life like champions. That's how you'll make it. Remember children; remember all things that ya Mama used to say". With that mama gasped her last breath, gathered her legs together like a lady and died. It was so peaceful. No ambulance, no police officer, only the hospice and the mortician who were family themselves. We all watched as our mania slept into silence.

I had the grand honor of taking care of Mama in her final days. I also placed her on the mortician's stretcher and placed her winning sheet over her lifeless frame. All of the men-folk in the neighborhood and the family marched her to the hearse. I quietly whispered, "Mama it's been an honor to serve", as I closed the door. The sky received her spirit with lightning gracing the clouds. We watched the car drive away slowly. It was over now. It was the end of a wonderful life; an era of knowledge. We did not know it, but we were about to enter a new phase in our lives, to test out what we had been taught. I thought to myself, "How can we forget you Mama? There is no way. We cannot forget all the things that our *Mama Used to Say*.

Benediction-

Now unto God who is both able and willing to keep all of us from falling.

Be the power and the Glory henceforth and forevermore, we praise your most holy name.

Thanks to the Kingdom from which your son, stands. It is in his name we pray.

-Amen